W. A. MOZART

Twelve Duets for Two French Horns K.487

PLAYBACK+
Speed • Pitch • Balance • Loop

To access audio, visit:
www.halleonard.com/mylibrary

Enter Code
5527-3453-1363-8634

ISBN 978-1-59615-364-6

Music Minus One

EXCLUSIVELY DISTRIBUTED BY

HAL•LEONARD®

Visit Hal Leonard Online at
www.halleonard.com

World headquarters, contact:
Hal Leonard
7777 West Bluemound Road
Milwaukee, WI 53213
Email: info@halleonard.com

In Europe, contact:
Hal Leonard Europe Limited
1 Red Place
London, W1K 6PL
Email: info@halleonardeurope.com

In Australia, contact:
Hal Leonard Australia Pty. Ltd.
4 Lentara Court
Cheltenham, Victoria, 3192 Australia
Email: info@halleonard.com.au

W. A. MOZART

Twelve Duets for Two French Horns K.487

4   No. 1 - Allegro, Horn in F

5   No. 2 - Menuetto, Horn in E♭

6   No. 3 - Andante, Horn in F

7   No. 4 - Polonaise, Horn in F

8   No. 5 - Larghetto, Horn in D

8   No. 6 - Menuetto, Horn in E, Horn in E♭

10   No. 7 - Adagio, Horn in F

10   No. 8 - Allegro, Horn in E♭

12   No. 9 - Menuetto, Horn in E♭

13   No. 10 - Andante, Horn in F

14   No. 11 - Menuetto, Horn in G

15   No. 12 - Allegro, Horn in E♭

1 ALLEGRO

W.A. MOZART
(1756-1791)

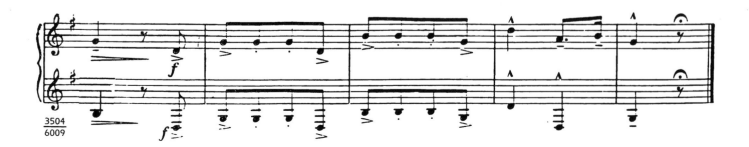

3504
6009

2 MENUETTO

Horn in Eb

Horn in Eb

TRIO

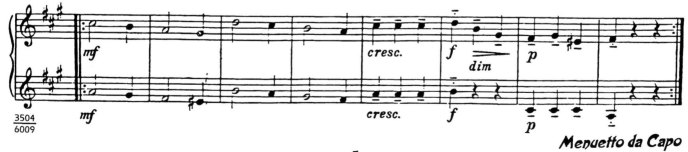

3504
6009

Menuetto da Capo

3 ANDANTE

1. Horn in F

2. Horn in F

4 POLONAISE

Horn in F

Horn in F

(Tempo I)

3504
6009

5 LARGHETTO

Horn in D

Horn in D

6 MENUETTO

Horn in E

Horn in E

3504
6009

TRIO

Horn in Eb

Horn in Eb

mf espr.

7 ADAGIO

Horn in F

Horn in F

8 ALLEGRO

Horn in Eb

Horn in Eb

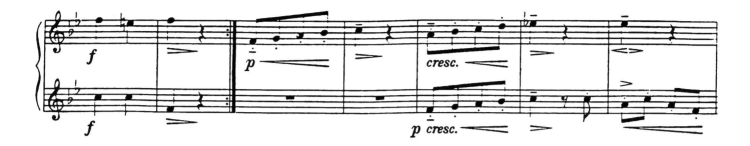

9 MENUETTO

Horn in Eb

Horn in Eb

TRIO

Menuetto da Capo

10 ANDANTE

Horn in F

Horn in F

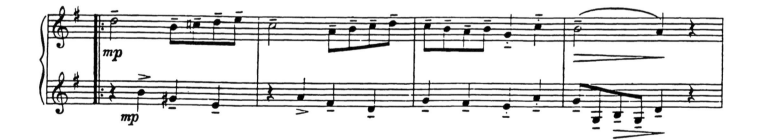

3504
6009

11 MENUETTO

Horn in G

Horn in G

TRIO

3504
6009

Menuetto da Capo

12 ALLEGRO

Horn in Eb

Horn in Eb

3504
6009

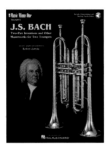

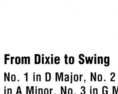